ŒDIPUS TYRANNUS;

OR,

SWELLFOOT the TYRANT.

𝕬 𝕿𝖗𝖆𝖌𝖊𝖉𝖞.

IN TWO ACTS.

TRANSLATED FROM THE ORIGINAL DORIC.

————— Choose Reform or civil-war,
When thro' thy streets, instead of hare with dogs,
A CONSORT-QUEEN shall hunt a KING with hogs,
Riding on the IONIAN MINOTAUR.

LONDON:

PUBLISHED FOR THE AUTHOR,

BY J. JOHNSTON, 98, CHEAPSIDE, AND SOLD BY
ALL BOOKSELLERS.

1820.

ADVERTISEMENT.

[BY SHELLEY.]

———◆———

THIS TRAGEDY is one of a triad, or system of three Plays, (an arrangement according to which the Greeks were accustomed to connect their Dramatic representations,) elucidating the wonderful and appalling fortunes of the SWELLFOOT dynasty. It was evidently written by some *learned Theban*, and, from its characteristic dullness, apparently before the duties on the importation of *Attic salt* had been repealed by the Bœotarchs. The tenderness with which he treats[1] the PIGS proves him to have been a *sus Bœotiæ*; possibly *Epicuri de grege porcus*; for, as the poet observes,

"A fellow feeling makes us wond'rous kind."

No liberty has been taken with the translation of this remarkable piece of antiquity, except the suppressing a seditious and blasphemous Chorus of the Pigs and Bulls at the last act. The word Hoydipouse, (or more properly Œdipus,) has been rendered literally SWELLFOOT, without its having been conceived necessary to determine whether a swelling of the hind or the fore feet of the Swinish Monarch is particularly indicated.

Should the remaining portions of this Tragedy be found, entitled, "*Swellfoot in Angaria,*" and "*Charité,*" the Translator might be tempted to give them to the reading Public.

---

[1] In Mrs. Shelley's editions the word here is *beats*. Mr. Rossetti, in printing *treats*, says the word is *beats* "in previous texts;" but it is not so in Shelley's own edition, as might be inferred: in that, it is duly printed *treats*.

DRAMATIS PERSONÆ.

TYRANT SWELLFOOT, King of Thebes.

IONA TAURINA, his Queen.

MAMMON, Arch-Priest of Famine.

PURGANAX[1]
DAKRY[2] } Wizards, Ministers of SWELLFOOT.
LAOCTONOS[3]

The GADFLY	MOSES, the Sow-gelder.
The LEECH	SOLOMON, the Porkman.
The RAT	ZEPHANIAH, Pig Butcher.
The MINOTAUR.	

Chorus of the Swinish Multitude.

GUARDS, ATTENDANTS, PRIESTS, &c., &c.

---

[1] Purganax is of course Lord Castlereagh. Mr. Rossetti, because the name is derived from πύργος (castle) and ἄναξ (King), sees fit to alter the spelling to *Pyrganax* throughout the poem, remarking that that "is the proper spelling." Surely when there are scholars who spell even *Olympus* with a *u* instead of a *y*, it must be a matter of opinion what is the "proper spelling" of Shelley's word; and surely, if he chose to give an English *u* as the equivalent for a Greek *v*, his predilection should be respected.

[2] Dakry represents Lord Eldon.

[3] Laoctonos is Wellington.

ŒDIPUS TYRANNUS,

A TRAGEDY.

In Two Acts.

SCENE.——THEBES.

ACT I.

SCENE I.—*A magnificent Temple, built of thigh-bones and death's heads, and tiled with scalps. Over the Altar the statue of Famine, veiled; a number of boars, sows, and sucking pigs, crowned with thistle, shamrock, and oak, sitting on the steps, and clinging round the altar of the Temple.*

Enter Swellfoot, *in his Royal robes, without perceiving the* Pigs.

Swellfoot.

Thou supreme Goddess! by whose power divine
These graceful limbs are clothed in proud array

(He contemplates himself with satisfaction.)

Of gold and purple, and this kingly paunch
Swells like a sail before a favouring breeze,
And these most sacred nether promontories 5
Lie satisfied with layers of fat; and these

B 2

Bœotian cheeks, like Egypt's pyramid,
(Nor with less toil were their foundations laid,[1])
Sustain the cone of my untroubled brain,
That point, the emblem of a pointless nothing!   10
Thou to whom Kings and laurelled Emperors,
Radical-butchers, Paper-money-millers,
Bishops and deacons, and the entire army
Of those fat martyrs to the persecution
Of stifling turtle-soup, and brandy-devils,   15
Offer their secret vows! Thou plenteous Ceres
Of their Eleusis, hail![2]

THE SWINE.

Eigh! eigh! eigh! eigh!

SWELLFOOT.

Ha! what are ye,
Who, crowned with leaves devoted to the Furies,
Cling round this sacred shrine?

SWINE.

Aigh! aigh! aigh!

SWELLFOOT.

What! ye that are
The very beasts that offered at her altar   20

---

[1] See Universal History for an account of the number of people who died, and the immense consumption of garlick by the wretched Egyptians, who made a sepulchre for the name as well as the bodies of their tyrants. [SHELLEY'S NOTE.]

[2] In case some future editor may see cause to "reform" the metre of this interrupted portion of Swellfoot's speech, it may be worth while to note that it is not defective: the three utterances of The Swine are merely inarticulate interruptions (for which reason they are not taken into account in numbering the lines); and it will be observed that, eliminating these grunts, the iambic lines of Swellfoot's speech are unbroken and unimpeachable.

With blood and groans, salt-cake, and fat, and inwards
Ever propitiate her reluctant will
When taxes are withheld?

SWINE.

Ugh! ugh! ugh!

SWELLFOOT.

What! ye who grub
With filthy snouts my red potatoes up
In Allan's rushy bog? Who eat the oats   25
Up, from my cavalry in the Hebrides?
Who swill the hog-wash soup my cooks digest
From bones, and rags, and scraps of shoe-leather,
Which should be given to cleaner Pigs than you?

THE SWINE.

Semichorus I.

The same, alas! the same;   30
Though only now the name
    Of pig remains to me.

Semichorus II.

If 'twere your kingly will
Us wretched swine to kill,
    What should we yield to thee?   35

SWELLFOOT.

Why skin and bones, and some few hairs for mortar.

CHORUS OF SWINE.

I have heard your Laureate sing,
That pity was a royal thing;
Under your mighty ancestors, we pigs

Were bless'd as nightingales on myrtle sprigs,   40
Or grass-hoppers that live on noon-day dew,
And sung, old annals tell, as sweetly too,
But now our styes are fallen in, we catch
   The murrain and the mange, the scab and itch;
Sometimes your royal dogs tear down our thatch,   45
   And then we seek the shelter of a ditch;
Hog-wash or grains, or ruta baga, none
Has yet been ours since your reign begun.

FIRST SOW.

My pigs, 'tis in vain to tug.

SECOND SOW.

I could almost eat my litter.   50

FIRST PIG.

I suck, but no milk will come from the dug.

SECOND PIG.

Our skin and our bones would be bitter.

THE BOARS.

We fight for this rag of greasy rug,
   Though a trough of wash would be fitter.

SEMICHORUS.

Happier swine were they than we,   55
Drowned in the Gadarean sea—
I wish that pity would drive out the devils,
Which in your royal bosom hold their revels,
And sink us in the waves of thy[1] compassion!
Alas! the Pigs are an unhappy nation!   60

      [1] In Mrs. Shelley's edition, *your*.

Now if your Majesty would have our bristles
  To bind your mortar with, or fill our colons
With rich blood, or make brawn out of our gristles,
  In policy—ask else your royal Solons—
You ought to give us hog-wash and clean straw,   65
And styes well thatched; besides it is the law !

SWELLFOOT.

This is sedition, and rank blasphemy!
Ho! there, my guards!

Enter a GUARD.

GUARD.

Your sacred Majesty.

SWELLFOOT.

Call in the Jews, Solomon the court porkman,
Moses the sow-gelder, and Zephaniah   70
The hog-butcher.[1]

GUARD.

They are in waiting, Sire.

Enter SOLOMON, MOSES, *and* ZEPHANIAH.

SWELLFOOT.

Out with your knife, old Moses, and spay those sows,
    (*The pigs run about in consternation*)
That load the earth with pigs; cut close and deep,
Moral restraint I see has no effect,
Nor prostitution, nor our own example,   75
Starvation, typhus-fever, war, nor prison—
This was the art which the arch-priest of Famine

---

[1] In Shelley's edition and all others known to me the words *the hog-butcher,* clearly the complement of line 71, are printed at the end of line 70.

Hinted at in his charge to the Theban clergy—
Cut close and deep, good Moses.

MOSES.

Let your Majesty

Keep the boars quiet, else——

SWELLFOOT.

Zephaniah, cut   80
That fat hog's throat, the brute seems overfed;
Seditious hunks! to whine for want of grains.

ZEPHANIAH.

Your sacred Majesty, he has the dropsy;—
We shall find pints of hydatids in's liver,
He has not half an inch of wholesome fat   85
Upon his carious ribs——

SWELLFOOT.

'Tis all the same,
He'll serve instead of riot money, when
Our murmuring troops bivouaque in Thebes' streets;
And January winds, after a day
Of butchering, will make them relish carrion.   90
Now, Solomon, I'll sell you in a lump
The whole kit of them.

SOLOMON.

Why, your Majesty,

I could not give——

SWELLFOOT.

Kill them out of the way,
That shall be price enough, and let me hear
Their everlasting grunts and whines no more!   95

(*Exeunt, driving in the swine.*)

Enter MAMMON, *the Arch-Priest; and* PURGANAX,[1] *Chief of
the Council of Wizards.*

PURGANAX.

The future looks as black as death, a cloud,
Dark as the frown of Hell, hangs over it—
The troops grow mutinous—the revenue fails—
There's something rotten in us—for the level
Of the State slopes, its very bases topple,   100
The boldest turn their backs upon themselves!

MAMMON.

Why what's the matter, my dear fellow, now?
Do the troops mutiny?—decimate some regiments;
Does money fail?—come to my mint—coin paper,
Till gold be at a discount, and ashamed   105
To show his bilious face, go purge himself,
In emulation of her vestal whiteness.

PURGANAX.

Oh, would that this were all! The oracle!!

MAMMON.

Why it was I who spoke that oracle,
And whether I was dead drunk or inspired,   110
I cannot well remember; nor, in truth,
The oracle itself!

PURGANAX.

The words went thus[2] :—
" Bœotia, choose reform or civil war!

---

[1] In Shelley's edition, in this stage direction, we read *Arch Priest*, in two words without a hyphen, and there is no comma at *Purganax*. *Arch-Priest* with the hyphen is usually found, as in the list of *dramatis personæ*, as in line 126 of this Act (see next page), and in the stage direction at the opening of Scene II of the Second Act.

[2] See supplementary note, at the end of the poem.

" When through thy streets, instead of hare with dogs,
" A Consort Queen shall hunt a King with hogs,   115
" Riding on the Ionian Minotaur."

MAMMON.

Now if the oracle had ne'er foretold
This sad alternative, it must arrive,
Or not, and so it must now that it has,
And whether I was urged[1] by grace divine,   120
Or Lesbian liquor to declare these words,
Which must, as all words must, be false or true;
It matters not: for the same power made all,
Oracle, wine, and me and you—or none—
'Tis the same thing. If you knew as much[2]   125
Of oracles as I do——

PURGANAX.

          You arch-priests
Believe in nothing; if you were to dream
Of a particular number in the Lottery,
You would not buy the ticket?[3]

MAMMON.

          Yet our tickets
Are seldom blanks. But what steps have you taken ? 130
For prophecies when once they get abroad,
Like liars who tell the truth to serve their ends,
Or hypocrites who, from assuming virtue,
Do the same actions that the virtuous do,
Contrive their own[4] fulfilment. This Iona——   135

[1] In Shelley's edition, *urg'd*.
[2] So in Shelley's and Mrs. Shelley's editions : Mr. Rossetti prints the line

'Tis the same thing. If you *but* knew as much;

but surely, if it be admissible to alter the line at all for the sake of the metre, it would be safer to give the initial word *It* in full, instead of abbreviating it.

[3] In Shelley's edition there is a note of interrogation here : Mrs. Shelley changes the sense by substituting a note of exclamation; and Mr. Rossetti rejects that for a full-stop.

[4] The word *own* is not in Shelley's edition or Mrs. Shelley's second of 1839, wherein the poem was first reprinted; but it appears in some of her later editions.

Well—you know what the chaste Pasiphae did,
Wife to that most religious King of Crete,
And still how popular the tale is here ;
And these dull swine of Thebes boast their descent
From the free Minotaur. You know they still   140
Call themselves Bulls, though thus degenerate,
And every thing relating to a bull
Is popular and respectable in Thebes.
Their arms are seven bulls in a field gules,[1]
They think their strength consists in eating beef,—   145
Now there were danger in the precedent
If Queen Iona——

PURGANAX.

I have taken good care
That shall not be. I struck the crust o' the earth
With this enchanted rod, and Hell lay bare !
And from a cavern full of ugly shapes,   150
I chose a LEECH, a GADFLY, and a RAT.
The gadfly was the same which Juno sent
To agitate Io,[2] and which Ezechiel* mentions
That the Lord whistled for out of the mountains
Of utmost Æthiopia,[3] to torment   155
Mesopotamian Babylon. The beast

* And the Lord whistled for the gadfly out of Æthiopia, and for the bee of Egypt, &c.—EZECHIEL. [SHELLEY'S NOTE, in which, in his edition, Æthiopia is spelt Œthiopia.]

[1] Has this curious piece of heraldry reference to the six leopards and the lion rampant which figure on the Royal Standard ?

[2] Shelley's reference here to the *Prometheus Bound* is very curiously printed in the original edition, namely thus,—" The prometheus bound of Æschylus." This probably arose from the effect, on an ignorant compositor, of Shelley's practice of writing titles without either inverted commas or marks to signify Italics, and his fre-quent use of a small *p* rather larger than usual to serve as a capital.

[3] Curiously enough, in Shelley's edition, this word is here spelt in the orthodox way, *Ethiopia*. I believe Shelley habitually wrote it with an Æ diphthong ; and in those instances in which I have seen the MS. his Æ diphthong capital is absolutely indistinguishable from Œ diphthong,—which fact would account for the very curious orthography in his note, above.

Has a loud trumpet like the Scarabee,
His crookèd tail is barbed with many stings,
Each able to make a thousand wounds, and each
Immedicable ; from his convex eyes   160
He sees fair things in many hideous shapes,
And trumpets all his falsehood to the world.
Like other beetles he is fed on dung—
He has eleven feet with which he crawls,
Trailing a blistering slime, and this foul beast   165
Has tracked Iona from the Theban limits,
From isle to isle, from city unto city,
Urging her flight from the far Chersonese
To fabulous Solyma, and the Ætnean Isle,
Ortygia, Melite, and Calypso's Rock,   170
And the swart tribes of Garamant and Fez,
Æolia and Elysium, and thy shores,
Parthenope, which now, alas ! are free !
And through the fortunate Saturnian land,
Into the darkness of the West.

MAMMON.

                        But if   175
This Gadfly should drive Iona hither ?[1]

PURGANAX.

Gods ! what an *if !* but there is my grey RAT :
So thin with want, he can crawl in and out
Of any narrow chink and filthy hole,
And he shall creep into her dressing-room,   180
And———

---

[1] So in Shelley's and Mrs. Shelley's editions ; but, as the line is short and defective, it seems most probable that the right reading would be *Queen Iona*, as in line 193. It might, however, equally well be *This Gadfly now should drive, &c.* Mr. Rossetti prints *hither* in Italics ; but that does not mend the line. He suggests the insertion of *but* after *should ;* but that would clash with *But* in the previous line.

MAMMON.

My dear friend, where are your wits ? as if
She does not always toast a piece of cheese
And bait the trap ? and rats, when lean enough
To crawl through *such* chinks———

PURGANAX.

              But my LEECH—a leech
Fit to suck blood, with lubricous round rings,   185
Capaciously expatiative, which make
His little body like a red balloon,
As full of blood as that of hydrogene,
Sucked from men's hearts ; insatiably he sucks
And clings, and pulls—a horse-leech, whose deep maw
The plethoric King Swellfoot could not fill,   191
And who, till full, will cling for ever.

MAMMON.

                  This
For Queen Iona might suffice, and less ;
But 'tis the swinish multitude I fear,
And in that fear I have———

PURGANAX.

         Done what ?

MAMMON.

             Disinherited   195
My eldest son Chrysaor, because he
Attended public meetings, and would always
Stand prating there of commerce, public faith,
Economy, and unadulterate coin,
And other topics, ultra-radical;   200
And have entailed my estate, called the Fool's Paradise,
And funds in fairy-money, bonds, and bills,

Upon my accomplished daughter Banknotina,
And married her to the gallows.[1]

PURGANAX.

A good match!

MAMMON.

A high connection, Purganax. The bridegroom   205
Is of a very ancient family,
Of Hounslow Heath, Tyburn, and the New Drop,
And has great influence in both Houses;—Oh!
He makes the fondest husband; nay, *too* fond,—
New married people should not kiss in public;   210
But the poor souls love one another so!
And then my little grandchildren, the gibbets,
Promising children as you ever saw,—
The young playing at hanging, the elder learning
How to hold radicals. They are well taught too,   215
For every gibbet says its catechism
And reads a select chapter in the Bible
Before it goes to play.

(*A most tremendous humming is heard.*)

PURGANAX.

Ha! what do I hear?

Enter the GADFLY.[2]

MAMMON.

Your Gadfly, as it seems, is tired of gadding.

---

[1] If one should marry a gallows, and beget young gibbets, I never saw
one so prone.—CYMBELINE. [SHELLEY'S NOTE.]

[2] So in Shelley's edition: in Mrs.
Shelley's the stage direction is *Enter*   *Gadfly:* in Mr. Rossetti's it is *Enter
Gadfly followed by Leech and Rat.*

GADFLY.

Hum! hum! hum!   220
From the lakes of the Alps, and the cold grey scalps
    Of the mountains, I come
Hum! hum! hum!
From Morocco and Fez, and the high palaces
    Of golden Byzantium;   225
From the temples divine of old Palestine,
    From Athens and Rome,
    With a ha! and a hum!
    I come! I come!

    All inn-doors and windows   230
        Were open to me:
    I saw all that sin does,
        Which lamps hardly see
That burn in the night by the curtained bed,—
The impudent lamps! for they blushed not red,   235
        Dinging and singing,
        From slumber I rung her,
    Loud as the clank of an ironmonger;
            Hum! hum! hum!

    Far, far, far!   240
With the trump of my lips, and the sting at my hips,
    I drove her—afar!
    Far, far, far!
From city to city, abandoned of pity,
    A ship without needle or star;—   245
Homeless she past, like a cloud on the blast,
    Seeking peace, finding war;—
    She is here in her car,
    From afar, and afar;—
            Hum! hum!   250

I have stung her and wrung her,
    The venom is working;—
And if you had hung her
    With canting and quirking,
She could not be deader than she will be soon;—   255
I have driven her close to you, under the moon,
    Night and day, hum! hum! ha!
I have hummed her and drummed her
From place to place, till at last I have dumbed her,[1]
        Hum! hum! hum!   260

LEECH.[2]

    I will suck
    Blood or muck!
The disease of the state is a plethory,
Who so fit to reduce it as I?

RAT.

I'll slily seize and   265
Let blood from her weasand,—
Creeping through crevice, and chink, and cranny,
With my snakey tail, and my sides so scranny.

PURGANAX.

Aroint ye! thou unprofitable worm!
                        (to the Leech)
And thou, dull beetle, get thee back to hell!   270
                        (to the Gadfly)
To sting the ghosts of Babylonian kings,
And the ox-headed Io——

---

[1] In Shelley's edition, in these two lines, we read *humm'd*, *drumm'd* and *dumb'd*,—an exception to his practice, but possibly intentional here.
[2] It seems to me that the missing stage direction to account for the presence of the Leech and the Gadfly should be here; but it is in all probability owing to Shelley's own oversight that we do not read *Enter the Leech and the Rat*.

SWINE (*within*).

Ugh, ugh, ugh!

Hail! Iona the divine,
We will be no longer swine,
But bulls with horns and dewlaps.

RAT.

For,   275

You know, my lord, the Minotaur——

PURGANAX (*fiercely*).

Be silent! get to hell! or I will call
The cat out of the kitchen.[1] Well, Lord Mammon,
This is a pretty business.

(*Exit the Rat.*)

MAMMON.

I will go
And spell some scheme to make it ugly then.——   280

(*Exit.*)

Enter SWELLFOOT.

SWELLFOOT.

She is returned! Taurina is in Thebes
When Swellfoot wishes that she were in hell!
Oh, Hymen, clothed in yellow jealousy,
And waving o'er the couch of wedded kings
The torch of discord with its fiery hair;   285
This is thy work, thou patron saint of queens!
Swellfoot is wived! though parted by the sea,
The very name of wife had conjugal rights;
Her cursèd image ate, drank, slept with me,

---

[1] This full-stop is wanting in Shelley's edition; but there is a long space between the words *kitchen* and *Well;* and the omission was obviously accidental.

C

And in the arms of Adiposa oft   290
Her memory has received a husband's——

A loud tumult, and cries of "Iona for ever!—No
Swellfoot!"

SWELLFOOT.

                                        Hark!
How the swine cry Iona Taurina;
I suffer the real presence; Purganax,
Off with her head!

PURGANAX.

                    But I must first impanel[1]
A jury of the pigs.

SWELLFOOT.

                    Pack them then.[2]   295

PURGANAX.

Or fattening some few in two separate styes,
And giving them clean straw, tying some bits
Of ribbon round their legs—giving their sows
Some tawdry lace, and bits of lustre glass,
And their young boars white and red rags, and tails   300
Of cows, and jay feathers, and sticking cauliflowers
Between the ears of the old ones; and when
They are persuaded, that by the inherent virtue
Of these things, they are all imperial pigs,
Good Lord! they'd rip each other's bellies up,   305
Not to say help us in destroying her.

---

[1] In Shelley's edition, *impannel.*
[2] To get over the defectiveness of metre here, Mr. Rossetti thinks *go pack them then* " would not be a very daring emendation." I should incline to *Well, pack them then,* as more probably what Shelley wrote.

SWELLFOOT.

This plan might be tried too ;—where's General
Laoctonos ?[1]

Enter LAOCTONOS *and* DAKRY.

It is my royal pleasure
That you, Lord General, bring the head and body,
If separate it would please me better, hither   310
Of Queen Iona.

LAOCTONOS.

That pleasure I well knew,
And made a charge with those battalions bold,
Called, from their dress and grin, the royal apes,
Upon the swine, who, in a hollow square
Enclosed her, and received the first attack   315
Like so many rhinoceroses, and then
Retreating in good order, with bare tusks
And wrinkled snouts presented to the foe,
Bore her in triumph to the public stye.
What is still worse, some sows upon the ground   320
Have given the ape-guards apples, nuts, and gin,
And they all whisk their tails aloft, and cry,
" Long live Iona! down with Swellfoot!"

PURGANAX.

Hark!

THE SWINE, *without*.

Long live Iona! down with Swellfoot!

---

[1] In Shelley's edition, and others   *Laoctonos* is printed as part of line
earlier than Mr. Rossetti's, the word   307.

DAKRY.

I

Went to the garret of the swineherd's tower,   325
Which overlooks the stye, and made a long
Harangue (all words) to the assembled swine,
Of delicacy, mercy, judgment, law,
Morals, and precedents, and purity,
Adultery, destitution, and divorce,   330
Piety, faith, and state necessity,
And how I loved the Queen!—and then I wept
With the pathos of my own eloquence,
And every tear turned to a mill-stone, which
Brained many a gaping pig,[1] and there was made   335
A slough of blood and brains upon the place,
Greased with the pounded bacon; round and round
The mill-stones[2] rolled, ploughing the pavement up,
And hurling sucking pigs into the air,
With dust and stones.——

Enter MAMMON.

MAMMON.

              I wonder that grey wizards
Like you should be so beardless in their schemes;   341
It had been but a point of policy
To keep Iona and the swine apart.
Divide and rule! but ye have made a junction
Between two parties who will govern you   345
But for my art.—Behold this BAG! it is
The poison BAG of that Green Spider huge,

---

[1] This grotesque version of the same imagery as is applied to Lord Eldon in *The Masque of Anarchy*, would serve, if need were, to identify that Lord Chancellor with Dakry :

His big tears, for he wept well,
Turned to mill-stones where they fell.
And the little children, who
Round his feet played to and fro,
Thinking every tear a gem,
Had their brains knocked out by them.

[2] In Shelley's edition, *millstones*, without a hyphen, though the word is spelt with a hyphen in line 334, and in the MS. of *The Masque of Anarchy*, in the passage just quoted.

On which our spies skulked in ovation through
The streets of Thebes, when they were paved with dead:
A bane so much the deadlier fills it now,   350
As calumny is worse than death,—for here
The Gadfly's venom, fifty times distilled,
Is mingled with the vomit of the Leech,
In due proportion, and black ratsbane, which
That very Rat, who, like the Pontic tyrant,   355
Nurtures himself on poison, dare not touch;—
All is sealed up with the broad seal of Fraud,
Who is the Devil's Lord High Chancellor,[1]
And over it the Primate of all Hell
Murmured this pious baptism:—" Be thou called   360
" The GREEN BAG; and this power and grace be thine:
" That thy contents, on whomsoever poured,
" Turn innocence to guilt, and gentlest looks
" To savage, foul, and fierce deformity.
" Let all baptized by thy infernal dew   365
" Be called adulterer, drunkard, liar, wretch!
" No name left out which orthodoxy loves,
" Court Journal or legitimate Review!—
" Be they called tyrant, beast, fool, glutton, lover
" Of other wives and husbands than their own—   370
" The heaviest sin on this side of the Alps!
" Wither they to a ghastly caricature
" Of what was human!—let not man or[2] beast
" Behold their face with unaverted eyes!
" Or hear their names with ears that tingle not   375
" With blood of indignation, rage, and shame!"—
This is a perilous liquor;—good my Lords.—

SWELLFOOT *approaches to touch the* GREEN BAG.

---

[1] *Cf. Masque of Anarchy* again:
Next came Fraud, and he had on,
Like Eldon, an ermine gown.

[2] So in Shelley's edition, of course
rightly; but *nor* in Mrs. Shelley's and
Mr. Rossetti's.

Beware ! for God's sake, beware !—if you should break
The seal, and touch the fatal liquor——

PURGANAX.

There,
Give it to me. I have been used to handle   380
All sorts of poisons. His dread Majesty[1]
Only desires to see the colour of it.

MAMMON.

Now, with a little common sense, my Lords,
Only undoing all that has been done,
(Yet so as it may seem we but confirm it,)   385
Our victory is assured. We must entice
Her Majesty from the stye, and make the pigs
Believe that the contents of the GREEN BAG
Are the true test of guilt or innocence.
And that, if she be guilty, 'twill transform her   390
To manifest deformity like guilt.
If innocent, she will become transfigured
Into an angel, such as they say she is ;
And they will see her flying through the air,
So bright that she will dim the noon-day sun ;   395
Showering down blessings in the shape of comfits.
This, trust a priest, is just the sort of thing
Swine will believe. I'll wager you will see them
Climbing upon the thatch of their low styes,
With pieces of smoked glass, to watch her sail   400
Among the clouds, and some will hold the flaps
Of one another's ears between their teeth,
To catch the coming hail of comfits in.
You, Purganax, who have the gift o' the gab,
Make them a solemn speech to this effect: 405

---

[1] In Shelley's edition *majesty*, in this one instance, is spelt with a small *m*.

I go to put in readiness the feast
Kept to the honour of our goddess Famine,
Where, for more glory, let the ceremony
Take place of the uglification of the Queen.

DAKRY (*to Swellfoot*).

I, as the keeper of your sacred conscience,   410
Humbly remind your Majesty that the care
Of your high office, as man-milliner
To red Bellona, should not be deferred.

PURGANAX.

All part, in happier plight to meet again.

[*Exeunt.*

END OF THE FIRST ACT.

ACT II.

SCENE I.—THE PUBLIC STYE.

The Boars in full Assembly.

Enter PURGANAX.

PURGANAX.

GRANT me your patience, Gentlemen and Boars,
Ye, by whose patience under public burthens
The glorious constitution of these styes
Subsists, and shall subsist. The lean-pig rates
Grow with the growing populace of swine,   5
The taxes, that true source of piggishness,
(How can I find a more appropriate term
To include religion, morals, peace, and plenty,
And all that fit Bœotia as a nation
To teach the other nations how to live ?)   10
Increase with piggishness itself; and still
Does the revenue, that great spring of all
The patronage, and pensions, and by-payments,
Which free-born pigs regard with jealous eyes,
Diminish, till at length, by glorious steps,   15
All the land's[1] produce will be merged in taxes,
And the revenue will amount to——nothing!
The failure of a foreign market for
Sausages, bristles, and blood-puddings,

---

[1] In Shelley's edition we read *lands* instead of *land's.*

And such home manufactures, is but partial;   20
And, that the population of the pigs,
Instead of hog-wash, has been fed on straw
And water, is a fact which is—you know—
That is—it is a state-necessity—
Temporary, of course. Those impious pigs,   25
Who, by frequent squeaks, have dared impugn[1]
The settled Swellfoot system, or to make
Irreverent mockery of the genuflexions
Inculcated by the arch-priest, have been whipt
Into a loyal and an orthodox whine.   30
Things being in this happy state, the Queen
Iona———

A loud cry from the PIGS.

She is innocent! most innocent!

PURGANAX.

That is the very thing that I was saying,
Gentlemen Swine; the Queen Iona being
Most innocent, no doubt, returns to Thebes,   35
And the lean sows and boars collect about her,
Wishing to make her think that WE believe
(I mean those more substantial pigs, who swill
Rich hog-wash, while the others mouth damp straw,)
That she is guilty; thus, the lean-pig faction   40
Seeks to obtain that hog-wash, which has been
Your immemorial right, and which I will
Maintain you in to the last drop of———

---

[1] So in Shelley's and Mrs. Shelley's editions; but there is clearly something wrong: Mr. Rossetti reconstructs the line thus:

Who *have*, by frequent squeaks, dared *to* impugn;

but the rhythm thus produced is not Shelley-like; nor can one see how such a line could have been misinterpreted into the line as printed in the text. I have little doubt that the very common printer's error of dropping some minor word was at the root of the imperfection; and should think the line was probably written thus:

Who, by *their* frequent squeaks, have dared impugn.

A BOAR.

(*interrupting him.*)

What
Does any one accuse her of?

PURGANAX.

Why, no one
Makes *any* positive accusation;—but   45
There were hints dropt, and so the privy wizards
Conceived that it became them to advise
His Majesty to investigate their truth;—
Not for his own sake; he could be content
To let his wife play any pranks she pleased,   50
If, by that sufferance, *he* could please the pigs;
But then he fears the morals of the swine,
The sows especially, and what effect
It might produce upon the purity and
Religion of the rising generation   55
Of sucking pigs, if it could be suspected
That Queen Iona————

(*A pause.*)

FIRST BOAR.

Well, go on; we long
To hear what she can possibly have done.

PURGANAX.

Why, it is hinted, that a certain bull—
Thus much is *known*:—the milk-white bulls that feed   60
Beside Clitumnus and the crystal[1] lakes
Of the Cisalpine mountains, in fresh dews
Of lotus-grass and blossoming asphodel,
Sleeking their silken hair, and with sweet breath

---

[1] In Shelley's edition, *chrystal.*

Loading the morning winds until they faint   65
With living fragrance, are so beautiful!——
Well, *I* say nothing;——but Europa rode
On such a one from Asia into Crete,
And the enamoured sea grew calm beneath
His gliding beauty. And Pasiphae,[1]   70
Iona's grandmother,——but *she* is innocent!
And that both you and I, and all assert.

FIRST BOAR.

Most innocent!

PURGANAX.

Behold this BAG; a bag——

SECOND BOAR.

Oh! no GREEN BAGS!! Jealousy's eyes are green,
Scorpions are green, and water-snakes, and efts,   75
And verdigris, and——————

PURGANAX.

             Honourable swine,
In piggish souls can prepossessions reign?
Allow me to remind you, grass is green—
All flesh is grass;—no bacon but is flesh—
Ye are but bacon. This divining BAG   80
(Which is not green, but only bacon colour)
Is filled with liquor, which if sprinkled o'er
A woman guilty of—we all know what—
Makes her so hideous, till she finds one blind
She never can commit the like again.   85
If innocent, she will turn into an angel,
And rain down blessings in the shape of comfits

---

[1] In Shelley's edition, *Pasiphæ.*

As she flies up to heaven. Now, my proposal
Is to convert her sacred Majesty
Into an angel, (as I am sure we shall do,)   90
By pouring on her head this mystic water.
            (*Shewing the Bag.*)
I know that she is innocent; I wish
Only to prove her so to all the world.

FIRST BOAR.

Excellent, just, and noble Purganax!

SECOND BOAR.

How glorious it will be to see her Majesty   95
Flying above our heads, her petticoats
Streaming like—like—like—

THIRD BOAR.

                Any thing.

PURGANAX.

                        Oh, no!
But like a standard of an admiral's ship,
Or like the banner of a conquering host,
Or like a cloud dyed in the dying day,   100
Unravelled on the blast from a white mountain;
Or like a meteor, or a war-steed's mane,
Or water-fall from a dizzy precipice
Scattered upon the wind.

FIRST BOAR.

                Or a cow's tail,——

SECOND BOAR.

Or *any thing*, as the learned Boar observed.   105

PURGANAX.

Gentlemen Boars, I move a resolution,
That her most sacred Majesty should be
Invited to attend the feast of Famine,
And to receive upon her chaste white body
Dews of Apotheosis from this BAG. 110

*A great confusion is heard of the PIGS OUT OF DOORS,
which communicates itself to those within. During the first
Strophe, the doors of the Stye are staved in, and a number
of exceedingly lean Pigs and Sows and Boars rush in.*

SEMICHORUS I.

No! Yes!

SEMICHORUS II.

Yes! No!

SEMICHORUS I.

A law!

SEMICHORUS II.

A flaw!

SEMICHORUS I.

Porkers, we shall lose our wash, 115'
Or must share it with the lean pigs!

FIRST BOAR.

Order! order! be not rash!
Was there ever such a scene, Pigs!

AN OLD SOW (*rushing in*).

I never saw so fine a dash
 Since I first began to wean pigs.   120

SECOND BOAR (*solemnly*).

The Queen will be an angel time enough.
I vote, in form of an amendment, that
Purganax rub a little of that stuff
Upon his face———

PURGANAX.

(*His heart is seen to beat through his waistcoat.*)

    Gods ! What would ye be at ?

SEMICHORUS I.

Purganax has plainly shown a   125
 Cloven foot and jack-daw feather.

SEMICHORUS II.

I vote Swellfoot and Iona
 Try the magic test together;
Whenever royal spouses bicker,
Both should try the magic liquor.   130

AN OLD BOAR (*aside*).

A miserable state is that of pigs,
 For if their drivers would tear caps and wigs,
The swine must bite each other's ear therefore.

AN OLD SOW (*aside*).

A wretched lot Jove has assigned to swine,
  Squabbling makes pig-herds hungry, and they dine 135
On bacon, and whip sucking-pigs the more.

CHORUS.

  Hog-wash has been ta'en away :
    If the Bull-Queen is divested,
  We shall be in every way
    Hunted, stript, exposed, molested ; 140
  Let us do whate'er we may,
    That she shall not be arrested.
QUEEN, we entrench you with walls of brawn,
  And palisades[1] of tusks, sharp as a bayonet :
Place your most sacred person here. We pawn 145
  Our lives that none a finger dare to lay on it.
    Those who wrong you, wrong us ;
    Those who hate you, hate us ;
    Those who sting you, sting us ;
    Those who bait you, bait us ; 150
The *oracle* is now about to be
Fulfilled by circumvolving destiny ;
Which says[2] : "Thebes, choose *reform* or *civil war*,
  " When through your streets, instead of hare with dogs,
  " A CONSORT QUEEN shall hunt a KING with hogs,
Riding upon the IONIAN MINOTAUR." 156

Enter IONA TAURINA.

IONA TAURINA (*coming forward*).

Gentlemen swine, and gentle lady-pigs,
The tender heart of every boar acquits

[1] In Shelley's edition, *pallisades*, with a double *l*. [2] See supplementary note at the end of the poem.

Their QUEEN, of any act incongruous
With native piggishness, and she reposing   160
With confidence upon the grunting nation,
Has thrown herself, her cause, her life, her all,
Her innocence, into their hoggish arms;
Nor has the expectation been deceived
Of finding shelter there. Yet know, great boars,   165
(For such who ever lives among you finds you,
And so do I) the innocent are proud!
I have accepted your protection only
In compliment of your kind love and care,
Not for necessity. The innocent   170
Are safest there where trials and dangers wait;
Innocent Queens o'er white-hot plough-shares tread
Unsinged, and ladies, Erin's laureate sings it,[1]
Decked with rare gems, and beauty rarer still,
Walked[2] from Killarney to the Giant's Causeway,   175
Through rebels, smugglers, troops of yeomanry,
White boys and orange boys, and constables,
Tithe-proctors, and excise people, uninjured!
Thus I!———
Lord PURGANAX, I do commit myself   180
Into your custody, and am prepared
To stand the test, whatever it may be!

PURGANAX.

This magnanimity in your sacred Majesty
Must please the pigs. You cannot fail of being
A heavenly angel. Smoke your bits of glass,   185
Ye loyal swine, or her transfiguration
Will blind your wondering eyes.

---

[1] Rich and rare were the gems she wore. *See Moore's Irish Melodies.*
[SHELLEY'S NOTE.]

[2] In Shelley's edition, *walk'd.*

AN OLD BOAR (*aside*).

> Take care, my Lord,
They do not smoke you first.

PURGANAX.

> At the approaching feast
Of Famine, let the expiation be.

SWINE.

Content! content!

IONA TAURINA (*aside*).

> I, most content of all,   190
Know that my foes even thus prepare their fall!

> [*Exeunt omnes.*

D

SCENE II.

The interior of the Temple of FAMINE. The statue of the Goddess, a skeleton clothed in party-coloured rags, seated upon a heap of skulls and loaves intermingled. A number of exceedingly fat Priests in black garments arrayed on each side, with marrow-bones and cleavers in their hands. A flourish of trumpets.

Enter MAMMON *as arch-priest,* SWELLFOOT, DAKRY, PURGANAX, LAOCTONOS, *followed by* IONA TAURINA *guarded. On the other side enter the* SWINE.

Chorus of PRIESTS,
Accompanied by the Court Porkman[1] on marrow-bones and cleavers.

GODDESS bare, and gaunt, and pale,
Empress of the world, all hail!
What though Cretans old called thee
City-crested Cybele?
We call thee FAMINE!   5
Goddess of fasts and feasts, starving and cramming;
Through thee, for emperors, kings, and priests and lords,

---

[1] This word is *Porkman* in all editions except that of Mr. Rossetti, who substitutes *Porkmen*. I cannot, however, think it safe to adopt either this or the alteration he makes in the scene-description,—the insertion of *Court Porkmen* so as to deprive the fat Priests of their marrow-bones and cleavers. I feel pretty sure that the picture Shelley had in his mind was one of Priests bearing marrow-bones and cleavers. What particular value he may have meant to attach to the phrase "accompanied by the Court Porkman on marrow bones and cleavers," is not very clear; but probably the idea was that the Court Porkman, as well as the Priests, both played and sang. The introduction of Court Porkmen in the plural is wholly inconsistent with the list of *dramatis personæ* and line 69 of Act I: in the one case we have "Solomon, the Porkman," and in the other "Solomon the court porkman,"—indicating, I think, that there was but one such dignitary in Thebes.

Who rule by viziers, sceptres, banknotes, words,
　　The earth pours forth its plenteous fruits,
　　Corn, wool, linen, flesh, and roots—　　　10
Those who consume these fruits thro' thee grow fat,
　Those who produce these fruits thro' thee grow lean,
Whatever change takes place, oh, stick to that!
　　And let things be as they have ever been;
　　　At least while we remain thy priests,　　　15
　　　And proclaim thy fasts and feasts!
Through thee the sacred SWELLFOOT dynasty
Is based upon a rock amid that sea
Whose waves are swine—so let it ever be!

SWELLFOOT, &c. seat themselves at a table, magnificently covered at the upper end of the temple. Attendants pass over the stage with hog-wash in pails. A number of pigs, exceedingly lean, follow them licking up the wash.

MAMMON.

I fear your sacred Majesty has lost　　　20
The appetite which you were used to have.
Allow me now to recommend this dish—
A simple kickshaw by your Persian cook,
Such as is served at the great King's second table.
The price and pains which its ingredients cost,　　　25
Might have maintained some dozen families
A winter or two—not more—so plain a dish
Could scarcely disagree.——

SWELLFOOT.

　　　　　　After the trial,
And these fastidious pigs are gone, perhaps
I may recover my lost appetite,—　　　30
I feel the gout flying about my stomach—
Give me a glass of Maraschino punch.

PURGANAX

(*Filling his glass, and standing up*).

The glorious constitution of the Pigs!

ALL.

A toast! a toast! stand up and three times three!

DAKRY.

No heel-taps—darken day-lights!—

LAOCTONOS.

                Claret, somehow,   35
Puts me in mind of blood, and blood of claret!

SWELLFOOT.

Laoctonos is fishing for a compliment,
But 'tis his due. Yes, you have drunk more wine,
And shed more blood than any man in Thebes.
                 (*To Purganax*)
For God's sake stop the grunting of those pigs!   40

PURGANAX.

We dare not, Sire, 'tis Famine's privilege.

CHORUS OF SWINE.

Hail to thee, hail to thee, Famine!
   Thy throne is on blood, and thy robe is of rags;
Thou devil which livest on damning;   44
   Saint of new churches, and cant, and GREEN BAGS,
Till in pity and terror thou risest,
Confounding the schemes of the wisest,
When thou liftest thy skeleton form,
   When the loaves and the skulls roll about,

We will greet thee—the voice of a storm　50
　Would be lost in our terrible shout!

Then hail to thee, hail to thee, Famine!
　Hail to thee, Empress of Earth!
When thou risest, dividing possessions;
When thou risest, uprooting oppressions;　55
　In the pride of thy ghastly mirth.
Over palaces, temples, and graves,
We will rush as thy minister-slaves,
Trampling behind in thy train,
Till all be made level again!　60

MAMMON.

I hear a crackling of the giant bones
Of the dread image, and in the black pits
Which once were eyes, I see two livid flames.
These prodigies are oracular, and show
The presence of the unseen Deity.　65
Mighty events are hastening to their doom!

SWELLFOOT.

I only hear the lean and mutinous swine
Grunting about the temple.

DAKRY.
　　　　　　　　In a crisis
Of such exceeding delicacy, I think
We ought to put her Majesty, the QUEEN,　70
Upon her trial without delay.

MAMMON.
　　　　　THE BAG
Is here.

PURGANAX.

I have rehearsed the entire scene
With an ox bladder and some ditch-water,
On Lady P.—it cannot fail.

(*Taking up the bag*)

           Your Majesty (*to Swellfoot*)
In such a filthy business had better   75
Stand on one side, lest it should sprinkle you,
A spot or two on me would do no harm,
Nay, it might hide the blood, which the sad genius
Of the Green Isle has fixed, as by a spell,
Upon my brow—which would stain all its seas,   80
But which those seas could never wash away !

IONA TAURINA.

My Lord, I am ready—nay, I am impatient
To undergo the test.

*A graceful figure in a semi-transparent veil passes unno-
ticed through the Temple ; the word LIBERTY is seen
through the veil, as if it were written in fire upon its forehead.
Its words are almost drowned in the furious grunting of the
Pigs, and the business of the trial. She kneels on the steps
of the Altar, and speaks in tones at first faint and low,
but which ever become louder and louder.*

    Mighty Empress ! Death's white wife !
    Ghastly mother-in-law of life !   85
    By the God who made thee such,
    By the magic of thy touch,
    By the starving and the cramming,
Of fasts and feasts ! by thy dread self, O Famine !
I charge thee ! when thou wake the multitude,   90

Thou lead them not upon the paths of blood.
The earth did never mean her foison[1]
For those who crown life's cup with poison
Of fanatic rage and meaningless revenge—
　　But for those radiant spirits, who are still 　　95
The standard-bearers in the van of Change.
　　Be they th' appointed stewards, to fill
The lap of Pain, and Toil, and Age!—
Remit, O Queen! thy accustomed[2] rage!
Be what thou art not! In voice faint and low 　　100
FREEDOM calls *Famine*,—her eternal foe,
To brief alliance, hollow truce.—Rise now!

*Whilst the veiled Figure has been chaunting this strophe,
MAMMON, DAKRY, LAOCTONOS, and SWELLFOOT, have
surrounded IONA TAURINA, who, with her hands folded on
her breast, and her eyes lifted to Heaven, stands, as with
saint-like resignation, to wait the issue of the business, in
perfect confidence of her innocence.*

*PURGANAX, after unsealing the GREEN BAG, is gravely
about to pour the liquor upon her head, when suddenly the
whole expression of her figure and countenance changes; she
snatches it from his hand with a loud laugh of triumph, and
empties it over SWELLFOOT and his whole Court, who are
instantly changed into a number of filthy and ugly animals,
and rush out of the Temple. The image of FAMINE then
arises with a tremendous sound, the PIGS begin scrambling
for the loaves, and are tripped up by the skulls[3]; all those
who EAT the loaves are turned into BULLS, and arrange themselves quietly behind the altar. The image of FAMINE sinks
through a chasm in the earth, and a MINOTAUR rises.*

[1] In Shelley's edition, *foizon*, as in line 228 of the *Lines Written among the Euganean Hills*.
[2] In Shelley's edition, *accustom'd*.
[3] In Shelley's edition, *sculls*, in this instance; but, as the word is spelt *skulls* in his edition in the scene-description at the beginning of this scene, and also in line 49, I presume we should give the preference to *skulls*.

MINOTAUR.

I am the Ionian Minotaur, the mightiest
Of all Europa's taurine progeny—
I am the old traditional man-bull;   105
And from my ancestors having been Ionian,
I am called Ion, which, by interpretation,
Is JOHN; in plain Theban, that is to say,
My name's JOHN BULL; I am a famous hunter,
And can leap any gate in all Bœotia,   110
Even the palings of the royal park,
Or double ditch about the new enclosures ;
And if your Majesty will deign to mount me,
At least till you have hunted down your game,
I will not throw you.   115

IONA TAURINA.

(*During this speech she has been putting on boots and spurs,
and a hunting cap, buckishly cocked on one side, and tucking
up her hair, she leaps nimbly on his back.*)

Hoa ! hoa! tallyho ! tallyho! ho ! ho !
Come, let us hunt these ugly badgers down,
These stinking foxes, these devouring otters,
These hares, these wolves, these any thing but men.
Hey, for a whipper-in ! my loyal pigs,   120
Now let your noses be as keen as beagles,
Your steps as swift as greyhounds, and your cries
More dulcet and symphonious than the bells
Of village-towers, on sunshine holiday ;
Wake all the dewy woods with jangling music.   125
Give them no law (are they not beasts of blood ?)
But such as they gave you. Tallyho! ho !
Through forest, furze, and bog, and den, and desart,
Pursue the ugly beasts ! tallyho ! ho !

Full Chorus of IONA *and the* SWINE.

  Tallyho! tallyho!   130
Through rain, hail, and snow,
Through brake, gorse, and briar,
Through fen, flood, and mire,
  We go! we go!

  Tallyho! tallyho!   135
Through pond, ditch, and slough,
Wind them, and find them,
Like the Devil behind them,
  Tallyho! tallyho!

(*Exeunt, in full cry;* IONA *driving on the* SWINE, *with the empty* GREEN BAG.)

THE END.

[OF ŒDIPUS TYRANNUS.]

.

The imprint of *Œdipus Tyrannus* is as follows :—

"C. F. SEYFANG, Printer, 57, Fleet Market."

[A very curious case of minute verbal and other variation is that of "the oracle," which first appears on the title-page of *Swellfoot*, and then occurs twice in the text of the poem. I have given it on the title-page precisely from Shelley's edition, in the minutest particulars: when PURGANAX utters it in Act I, beginning at line 112, it stands thus in the original edition:

> Bœotia, choose reform or civil war!
> When through the streets, instead of hare with dogs,
> A Consort Queen shall hunt a King with hogs,
> Riding on the Ionian Minotaur.

Here I have not thought it necessary to interfere with anything in the text except the word *the* in the second line of the oracle: that word, I have not the least doubt, is a misprint for *thy*; but I do not suppose the other variations were the printer's doing; and the note of exclamation at the end of the first line seems likely enough to have been deliberate. When the Chorus repeats the oracle in Act II, Sc. I, beginning at line 153, it runs, in Shelley's edition, thus:

> Thebes, choose *reform* or *civil war*,
> When through your streets instead of hare with dogs,
> A CONSORT QUEEN shall hunt a KING with hogs,
> Riding upon the IONIAN MINOTAUR.

In that case I have supplied, in the text, a comma after *streets* in the second line, because, whether Shelley or the printer dropped it, the omission must have been purely accidental, and damages the sense. But in regard to *your* for *thy* in the second line, and *upon* for *on* in the fourth, I should not doubt that those variations would have been left as they are, even if Shelley's attention had been called to them. If any one had asked him, "Why don't your people repeat the oracle correctly?"—he might fairly have answered, "Because real people don't repeat anything correctly in minute particulars": and, as regards the variations in the matter of italics, capitals, and so on, they probably place the stress more precisely where Shelley meant it to fall in each instance than would be the case if we ventured to print the oracle exactly alike in all three places. This case seems to me, without being of any intrinsic importance, to afford a good example of Shelley's un-minute way of work; and I think any textual critic who will take the trouble to compare the three versions, letter by letter, and point by point, will readily perceive as he goes on how little safety there can possibly be in "harmonizing" or "systematizing" the text of Shelley's poems.—H. B. F.]